Dissection Day

To Allie,

Dissection Day

Poems
Ally McGregor

MOON
TIDE PRESS

~ 2024 ~

Dissection Day

Editor-in-chief
Eric Morago

Editor Emeritus
Michael Miller

Marketing Specialist
Ellen Webre

Proofreader
Shelly Holder

Front cover art
Sophie Jane

Author photo
Ally McGregor

Book design
Michael Wada

Moon Tide logo design
Abraham Gomez

Dissection Day
is published by Moon Tide Press

Moon Tide Press
6709 Washington Ave. #9297
Whittier, CA 90608
www.moontidepress.com

FIRST EDITION

Printed in the United States of America

ISBN # 978-1-957799-15-5

For my fellow "mad" humans

Content Warning:
the following poems explore topics
that may be triggering to some readers,
including, but not limited to, allusions to suicide,
suicidal ideation, & self-harm.

Contents

I

Anatomical
Doll

II

Imaginary
Friends

III
Cradles
and Coffins

You may not believe in magic
but something very strange
is happening at this very moment.
Your head has dissolved into thin air
and I can see the rhododendrons
through your stomach.
It's not that you are dead
or anything dramatic like that,
it is simply that you are fading away
and I can't even remember your name.

— Leonora Carrington, *The Hearing Trumpet*

1
Anatomical
Doll

Hatching Hot Wheels

I regret not swallowing the toy
car the boy in grade school
would drive up & down
my body during recess—plastic
wheels speeding on the spaghetti
junctions of my spine, blowing
past stop signs in the creases
of my arms, refusing to use his blinker
as he did donuts around my thigh.
I once buried the car in the playground
sand, then sat on top of it—muffled
the engine with the frills of my skirt—
a mother bird suffocating her young.
He brought two the next day.

Now, cars still stalk me—
so close I could draw
on their dirty windows
with my fingertips—the drivers
decorating me with whistles
like flame stickers on my ribs—
impervious to the glares I carry
as pepper spray.
I want to regurgitate cars
in their faces—force-feed
vehicles down their throats
so I can joyride inside their stomachs,
floor-it up their esophagi

until panic nauseates them—
until they fear they might die—
because I've turned off my headlights
& it's night
& their houses are two blocks away
& they're alone.

But instead, I rev their satisfaction
with my reluctant smile—a checkered flag
that fuels them to speed away—
& they win the race
& they eat cereal out of gold trophies
& I'm back in grade school

being run over.

Pier Pressure

Fish don't use scales in the ocean—
      don't fillet their skin until they're thin—
until their bones sway with seafoam.
      I am not a fish.

I should only wear swimsuits at night—
      my supermassive stretch marks swallow
stars—cellulite never mistaken
      for constellations—the razor bumps
on my thighs a misleading
      guide for lost ships—directing
captains toward broken beacons.

No eyes can see through blubber—
      boiled until it can burn—
lighting a path in the darkness I hide in.

I don't have the confidence to flense
      the negative thoughts inside my head,
nor a swim bladder to keep myself afloat
      as I sink deep in critique.

But the tide pulls me—
        entering an aquatic amphitheater—
the waves clapping below me
        on a stage dusted with sand—
conch shell echoing in my ear:

now watch her collapse this pier
        with just the click of her heels.

Paper Faces

Collaging cutouts of smiles   from magazines—laugh lines

     carved deep into tired cheeks so cavernous

I can hear giggles   echoing off stalactite teeth—

     I feed my frowning face into the shredder,

skin blended to a smoothie I sip

          as I paste paper onto exposed muscle—

nostrils stuffed with tissues—wet glue dripping

          down my neck—

my brain perforated by paper cuts.

          With a new mouth, I swallow ink,

     let it burn inside my stomach

as I step outside—obey instructions on my eyelids:

     1.) when a stranger on the street asks

          how are you?

2.) cut out your tongue

3.) let the print painted

over your lips tell

a lie.

Cat's Cradle

The sidewalk is a runway I sprint down, my high heels clicking
like clocks counting down hours, minutes, seconds until nightfall—
until my shadow contorts into a cat—claws tapping on concrete,
whiskers twitching, ears vibrating at the ring of a faraway dinner bell.

The threads of my sweater catch on nails protruding from fences,
scarring my arms with bloody marks—olfactory tracking chips
for wolves to follow—my skin a perfume bottle nozzle spraying
trepidation into the air (it's vanilla-scented with notes of salt).

I can no longer distinguish plumes of car exhaust from hot breath
blown behind my ear—can't determine if I've stepped
in a puddle of water or drool.
Was that an ambulance siren or a howl behind me?

Streetlamps illuminate a pack of men blocking
a stairwell—their canines ricocheting moonlight.

My collar tightens—
the yarn twining
around my body until I'm folded
into a labyrinth—a cotton maze
for their gaze to permeate.

Eyes dilated in the darkness—apertures scanning for exits—
I flinch at their whistles: lullabies sung in pet cemeteries,
cradles & coffins sewn from domestic animal bones.

I recall the missing posters plastered to telephone poles—
the cats found dead each year on neighboring front lawns,
feline bodies splayed for involuntary vivisections—
& I wonder

am I wearing a cardigan
or an unzipped body bag?

Little Bo Peep

has lost her sheep—
they died together—
in their sleep.

The reaper arrived—
on his all-black trike—
to ferry their souls—
to the other side.

When the reaper inquired—
where are the souls—
Little Bo Peep replied—
Sir, I don't know.

He knew the solution—
a soul for a soul—
& with a grin—
smothered her with his cloak.

Her screams were muffled—
as they entered his lair—
& once inside—
he tied her to a chair.

With bony fingers—
he held her chin—
then swung his scythe—
to unzip her skin.

He stuffed her with cotton—
then sewed up her wounds—
seeing her in distress—
improved his foul mood.

With a bow on her head—
he placed her on a shelf—
as she sat there—
she wept to herself.

Alone with her thoughts—
she devised a plan—
the reaper would soon—
die again.

Ripping her stitches—
she was able to move—
stumbling in pain—
she left the room.

In the kitchen—
she found a knife—
but he had no heart—
knives wouldn't work right.

In the bathroom—
she saw the tub—
with gushing water—
she could create a flood.

But with no lungs—
he need not breathe—
& without his death—
she could never leave.

On her shelf—
she climbed back up—
to lie in wait—
for the reaper to come.

As he approached—
she jumped down—
& with a gasp—
he turned around.

She took her crook—
extending her limbs—
& with a swing—
decapitated him.

Picking up his skull—
from off the floor—
she carried it with her—
out the door.

Little Teapot

I've been tipped over—
poured out—
emptier now—
watered-down
to please the tongues
of those who could not drink
my soul steeped strong.

The Watermelon Tree

It sprouts from my mouth, climbs
  up my slick esophagus—a green
      sapling whose seed I was warned
              not to swallow, but I plugged my ears
                  with my fingers until it fertilized
              inside my stomach. You said you loved me
              despite the splinters, so I etched your name
      into my bark, let you saw my bleeding branches
to build us a house. I carved hearts from my wood
      each anniversary, whittled an engagement ring
              from my trunk—sap solidified
              to an amber gemstone—yet you
      were only a gardener watering
      me until I coiled around you.
Transfiguring to a striped beetle, you jammed
mandibles into my roots, feeding in secrecy
      so I blamed only myself for the holes
              that pierced me while you lounged
              underground—so deep my pleas
couldn't reach you. Each morning I harvest melons
      alone—pack their school lunches
      & sing them lullabies before bed.
I must water my daughters—warn them of the seeds
      already bobbing inside their bellies—of the bugs
              swinging baseball bats painted
                  to mimic sincerity.

25 Birthday Candles

drip wax down my face
    until I taste polka-dotted
drool decorating my lips.

I stabbed their pastel stems
    into my skull like malleable
scalpels—a lobotomy
    performed by Madame Tussaud—
because I wanted to slice
    myself as if I were a piece
of cake—inspect my organs
    for missing ingredients.

Did I add too much flour
    when rolling out my stomach?
How does one crack open a candied heart?
    Is it too late to add serotonin
sprinkles after I've baked my brain?

My eyes are rainbow lollipops stuck
    to fondant skin. Each year, they spiral
until I'm nauseated—vertigo visions
    playing in my mind as I rewind
my life like a VHS tape:

look, everyone, there I am,
    falling off the merry-go-round—
falling off the edge of the earth—
    falling into stars—into cuts, bruises,
& scars—falling apart—folding myself
    back together again like a napkin
on my lap I fidget with at the dinner table
    because I'm too afraid to excuse myself.

Sleepwalking With Scissors

Eyes closed in the kitchen,
only step on white tiles—
queen to f7,
music box ballerina pirouetting
on a 2-inch stage.
Don't you know ceramic
cracks like jawbreakers?

Feel the cold, cold metal sheathed
in a wooden drawer.
No, no, wrong sword,
drop the kids' scissors.
Slice yourself with those
& you'll spiral like a Slinky—
bleed pink instead of red.

You need scissors with the safety off.
Yes, those, the ones shaped like arteries
wrapped around a jump rope wrapped around a noose—
the ones mother told you not to run with.
Clutch them close to your heart.

Aren't you pleased you unlocked
the front door to hear the night breeze
sing through the holes in your head?

Skip through suburbia—
ants gripping your socks—
the sky wrapping you
in watercolor paper
drenched violet.

Trip & fall
through the sidewalk
damp with stardust.
Emerge on the other side
dressed in all black—
worms spelling eulogies
with their alphabet bodies.

At the chime of a church bell,
return home to find
your body asleep in bed—
breath interrupted
by a plastic handle
whistling from your throat.

Operation!

Passing scalpels to myself,

I play the part of nurse,

doctor, & patient—slice

my own body sleeping

on a yellow slab underneath

U.F.O. lights—remove   femurs with tweezers—

pluck a music box from my throat—

cradle my ice cream brain

bandaged with a warm waffle cone—

capture

my candy heart but drop it

before I can place it in a jar,

unable to wipe the sweat from my brow

before it drips

down

into my open incisions.

Floating above

my body, I am a balloon untethered

to the hum of surgical equipment

& *we're losing her* declaratives—

tampering with my own concentration—

hands shaking—

nose lit DANGER red—

until the error buzzer merges

with a flat-line ring.

Be Kind, Please Rewind

I regurgitate the pills I popped—
re-inflating as they exit my esophagus

to rest in their prescription bottle. I suck
tears back into my dry eyes & watch the slices

on my wrists suture themselves in slow-motion,
Band-Aids unpeeled in their packaging.

I walk backwards out of my apartment—
back to middle school where my fingers,

slammed inside lockers, un-bloom bruises.
Bullies remove their hands from my chest,

swallowing their spit from my hair
as they retreat & I rise from the linoleum floor.

I sit on the carpet of my childhood home—
soggy cereal hardening as the Sesame Street

theme song turns silent in its reversal
& I return the Blockbuster rental on time—

return to a time before the VHS ribbon
wrapped around my neck like a Mylar noose.

ll
Imaginary
Friends

Welcome to the Doll Psych Ward

Do dolls invite abuse, with their dent-able / heads, / those tight little painted-on or stitched-in / grins?

— Amy Gerstler

We've had our smiles unstitched
by childish hands who use our thread
to suture their own wounds.

We hurt more so they hurt less
yet they do not see how their blood
dyes our cotton brains red—
brains with stains
that must be bleached.

They lost our frontal lobes
in the washing machine,
but still, we must play pretend
that our skulls don't rattle
when we convulse.

These dollhouse walls are white.
These lacy dresses straitjackets.

We leap out of barred windows
each night hoping to die.
Every morning, nurses pop
plastic limbs back into place.
Our music box wails tinkle
throughout the halls.
Don't you hear it now?
The sound the ice cream truck made
as it jingled down your street?

And how it's the same tone
as the ambulance
bringing another one of us home?

Prozac in a PEZ Dispenser

I elongate my neck—
place Prozac in the pocket
of my esophagus—
feel its weight suspended
in my pink plastic body—
a prescription label raised on my ribs.
I wait patiently until it's time—
time to crack open my throat—
savor the pill on my tongue—
praying today I'll feel its effects
instead of simply sugar.

Inquiries from a Teddy Bear Inside a Washing Machine

Will this lavender water that
rushes through me as if it were spaghetti
escaping from a colander—detergent permeating
each cotton bone in my body—cleanse me of my sins?
Why did you leave me in the twilight park—after the sun
has closed the blinds, the stars too far to sound the alarm?
Who was that man in the van & why did he grab that woman so?
& why couldn't I move? Why did I just sit there as he alchemized
her to a doll, outlining her body in hopscotch chalk, ironing her skin
to the sidewalk? But what kind of witness would I make, my words
suffocated by apprehensive sutures sealing my mouth? Why wasn't
I stuffed with courage—the kind that rips blood-clotted Band-Aids
off quickly after a countdown—that tames a bicycle even with
purple knees—that swallows gum—that slams a bully's hand
inside a locker? When you remove me from this womb,
what should I do? My body is clean, but how
do I wash the scene from behind
my plastic eyes?

I Spy

During recess freedom—
hands cupped around my little eyes
like binoculars—

I'd survey the playground,
watch warthogs waiting in line
for water fountains—
toucans perched
on swaying swing sets—
snakes gliding down slides—
elephants shaking the ground
with each hopscotch jump—
ostracized ostriches
eating sandwiches together
in the bathroom.

Burying myself deep underground—
I squelched the pain
of isolation
with self-inflicted extinction—

watched the cold earth clump
in my eyes until I was blind—

wondered why
I was more worm
than girl—

until future archeologists found
me as a fossil, propped
my dusted body
inside a museum—
my name erased
by a scientific classification
etched in gold.

A Magician's Rabbit Resigns

Monsieur Magician,

Lately, you've only fed me thermometers—
the mercury a swelling applause rising
with my fever—cough syrup vanishing
from my throat like bitter
grape-flavored milk poured
from a baby doll's faux-filled bottle
before re-pooling in the spoon
held under my pink nose.

I've run out of ointment, ice bags,
& Band-Aids to apply,
my supply exhausted
from when I jumped
through hoops set ablaze—
caught playing cards
between my bleeding teeth—
acted as my own stunt double
shot out of a cannon—
had my heart pierced by swords—
was sawed in half, forced to watch
my fluffy tail writhe
on a wooden table
as you speared my head
with your magic wand
& held it like a scepter.

When you leave me in the velveteen darkness
of your top hat, its opening seems like the final spotlight—
a glowing halo I could wear if only I were to leap
through one last ring, my mind & body
joined together again as I hover
like a specter haunting an abandoned theater.

But if I rub my closed eyes hard enough,
I see stars through the light pollution—

& I will run while you bow for the crowd
& I will squint at sunlight instead of stage lights
& I will see the world without your illusions.

Crayon Copy

Our dandelion crowns
are pressed in picture frames—

stems we stole from bee
cavalries while they slept

so we could claim their royalty
like children dubbing each other

ephemeral rulers of the playground
until the bell rings & we forget

about our freedom—& though my mind
is no museum, no plaques under glass

cases to denote the importance
of that cheap umbrella either we

or the wind broke as the sky
coughed drops of rain & we stood there,

mouths agape, catching water like dogs
catching Frisbees—or that oven mitt

we accidentally tie-dyed with fire
when we forgot the cupcakes

were still baking—or those plastic
cups we captured cockroaches

in to teach them tricks—
& though you haven't bought

a ticket to these moments in months—
your shadow long since evaporated

from my walls—I drape paper atop
our memories, scribble on the parchment

with crayons until I've crafted Crayola
copies of you—replicas that can't replace,

yet still I papier-mâché myself
with the variegated pages, pretending

it's your warmth I feel
instead of glue.

Gummy Worms

They eat my intestines first—
saving my heart to savor later.
I pluck one from my lungs—
bite the pink half,
the remaining blue body
wiggling in my fingers.
The flavor tingles
my tongue—
the sour taste
of strawberries
on an abandoned
hopscotch court
rotting in the sun.

How Many Licks Does It Take to Get to the Center of a Poem?

Owls hovering above
our own sleeping heads,
we perch inside our brains—
pink tunnels housing
thought bubbles hovering
as if they were static
balloons stuck to ceilings.

We scavenge for bright ideas—
attempt to hoard light
bulbs like dragons
with vices for effervescence,
but instead tuck gloom
into our plumage.

Our minds are grape skies
where we fly, piercing
poems with our beaks:
stanzas sticky corn syrup stars—
alliteration the artificial
flavor of urgency—
assonance a moon
swallowed before chewing.

One, two, three
days we regurgitate
letters onto lollipop wrappers—

smear ink indistinguishable
from wet clumps of rodent hair
& bones—brilliance obscured
by bile—confectioners boiling
sugar glass that will shatter
once exposed to sunshine.

Sock Puppet Imposter

All the world's a stage in which I slip on tomatoes
launched by people pointing & laughing—a fool
tasked to dance while wearing weighted ballet shoes—
my brain cowering behind the curtains—my body
a carbonated can shaken to vomit alphabet soup—
letters spelling S.O.S—unable to converse
without convulsing in the spotlight.

I slip my hand into a tube sock—don an armored arm
of cotton—loose string intestines tickling my skin,
button eyes blinking, bedazzled lips sipping speech bubbles
as my fingers become a tongue—my nails brittle teeth
choking out consonants to the audience—
no nose to smell rotten fruit nor any ears
to echo taunting jeers.

A ventriloquist throwing my voice, I let a puppet
perfectly perform my life—sing my consciousness
to sleep so I can speak for once without stuttering—
my confidence a farce rehearsed to look improvised—
the panic striking my face replaced with a threaded
smile I couldn't have sewn myself.

Hiding behind felt & fuzz, catching roses
through a glove, I turn away from standing ovations—
swelling applause blocked by my internal monologue
screeching: *would they still clap if my hand were bare?*

Duck Duck Goose

El Dorado Duck Pond. Long Beach, California

Hypomania isn't happiness,

                  but the grass is edible

neon lime licorice   bladed

        around candy ants

           I was birthed   from the hole

of a rubber duck   I could breathe

           this pond water

        with my webbed lungs

if I wanted to

        (you're lucky I don't)

lay eggs in your brain

        (pinky promise I won't)

regurgitate you mealworms   & wet ferns

     from the terrarium   bubbles in my throat

          (they'll pop like mother's soap)

Stop telling me to pronounce my name

backwards

       to walk in a circle   counterclockwise

          tap me

       on the head instead

with a meat tenderizer

      balloon me with loaves of bread

from a fisherman's ripped pocket

          dip me in yolk

          roll me in flour

          prep me for dinner

with orange zest   shaved   on my goosebumps

      pluck my feathers   make me a quill

write with my blood

the line of a smile

```
    f           e
      r       l
        a g i
```

Humpty Dumpty

Humpty Dumpty sat on a wall / Humpty Dumpty had a great fall.

The king's men declared it a suicide—
secured the scene with yellow caution tape:
eggshells littering the sidewalk—
yolk brain cooking on sunny cement.

His family boiled at the news—
screamed their Humpty
was a straight-A student—
that he was the quarterback
of his high school football team—
that he attended church every Sunday.

The town declared it a tragedy—
the funeral presenting a slideshow
of Humpty volunteering
at the local animal shelter—
of him teaching children their ABC's—
of him smiling.

As they placed flowers
on his grave, they cried:
"We never knew—
never noticed the cracks he tried to glue.
   What could we have done—
     what could we have said
       to put our dear Humpty together again?"

To a Paper Doll Chain

I slice you with scissors—
　　follow the instructions
dictating where to cut: a circular head,
　　a sliver of thigh, a shard of arm—
but alarm materializes in the negative
　　spaces the holes leave behind.

It is through these holes I view you
　　as if peering into a kaleidoscope
devoid of color—a landscape
　　of paper snow swirling
at my ankles from all the times
　　I've shredded you
with my serrated fingers.

I fear you are my mirror—
　　that we are interchangeable,
you & I—
　　that as I carve
your body
　　I am mutilating
my own.

I don't want to hang our remains
　　like snowflakes strung
upon wintertime classroom windows—
　　doomed to drift to the linoleum floor

with a gust of wind—trampled
　　by children's muddy shoes
running inside from recess—
　　the teacher tossing our wet
parchment carcasses into the trash
　　once the school bell rings.

Let me instead clutch
　　our conjoined bodies
like a condensed
　　accordion—
cradle us close
　　to my heart,
yet inside
　　we multiply—
holding hands
　　infinitely.

Pinky Promise

In the moonlight, we lock pinkies—
two leopard slugs mating—
counterclockwise
swirling of skin
& bone—
promises hanging
from a thin mucus rope
suspended in the air.

Fragments from a Femme Enfant

Innocent as slowly licked lollipops
                    Pure as lamb fleece on a rotisserie
You brushed my skin gold   a mannequin
                    with metallic breasts
but pedestals have gravity   I fell
through your pupils   landed on a bouquet of brains

            You plucked
                            me an amygdala

        its petals lenticular
my name
        your name
                my name
            I'm a ghost haunting a gravestone
                    with an incorrect epitaph
I nursed poison   just to sleep
            You stole my corpse
buried it in a cradle   When your candles flicker
                it's me
            I map your home's intestines
You summon me to speak
                    & I vomit dreams
carve galaxies into trees
                    where we play hide-&-seek
            You always find me
        so I'll set fire to the leaves

watch the flames climb your wrists

           make snow angels in the debris

       of your phalanges

How will you write me into immortality

                with no hands?

III

Cradles
and Coffins

Recess

I am both the ant
& the magnifying glass—
insect exoskeleton turned
Sun-Maid raisin burned by a bright beam
that wishes it could void its direct order to kill.

Bubblegum Bubblegum in a Dish

With every mouth
murmuring money—
the codependency
of swallowing bubblegum whole
to keep a loose tooth
from falling out—
some call this
a wish.

The Tooth Fee

Over holey gums
I glide my tongue—
anxiously rolling my baby
teeth in my palm—
making my wish
before tucking
them under my pillow.

It's been only a moment
since the moon began mockingly
knocking on my open window—
its violent craters shallower
than those inside my minty mouth—
but I'm far too impatient
to wait for fairies to ferry
my enameled soul across
the Stream of Consciousness—
winged ants carrying polished
crumbs to a deity I cannot see,
yet somehow must believe in.

If I were to free my teeth
from their suffocated slumber—
thread a needle plucked
from mother's pin cushion
with a string of floss—
could I reattach them

with a few bloody stitches—
fill the vacuous void they left
behind—refuse the offer
of money, of the promise
that my adult teeth
will grow?

Or would I accidentally swallow them
like the pills on my bedside table
next to a glass of milk—
regurgitate them into my wet, quivering hands—
only to still find quarters
in their place?

Still Life Through a Kaleidoscope

Apple

seeds sprout from stomachs—
raindrops fall upward—
clocks lose summer leaves—
doctors rot at noon—
watch the blue worms chew.

Knife

reaper's apprentice—
a labyrinthine wrist—
swinging a weak scythe—
cellophane veins split—
red friendship bracelet.

Mirror

molting swan feathers—
sweating mourning dew—
plucked skin blooms violet—
parallax petals—
love me, love me not.

Doll

winding up the spine—
glass eyes filter salt—
teeth shatter vowels—
articulate tongue—
syllabic sorrow.

Pen

a diary key—
papier-mâché heart—
black bile ink leaking—
the bloodstream will feed—
please, no more leeches.

Bounce House Lungs

When having a panic attack
at a party, you must breathe
deeply—snort succulent frosting
flowers off the birthday cake precariously
perched on the edge of the table you're hiding
underneath, the scent settling to sweet floral
perfume—nostril hairs cutting the air
like knives slicing carbon dioxide
as you exhale sprinkles then inhale again—
suckle on nearby balloons—vacuum helium
with your throat, lungs inflating until
you begin to levitate—feet dangling
as if you had launched yourself
from a swing while gravity was switched
off—floating higher & higher
through layers of the atmosphere:
chasing cotton candy clouds—
giving directions to migrating birds—
beating airplanes in races—
popping the stratospheric bubble—
bumping into satellites—
knocking on the solar system's
front door—drifting by planets
waving with trays of warm muffins
to welcome you to the neighborhood.

Below, your missing face is printed
on milk cartons—newspaper headlines
pressing pedestrians for information
regarding your departure.

Above, you find peace
in being unable to breathe—
in forgoing control of your brain
to rotate in space—
Earth a snow globe you keep as a memory—
your body a music box
humming *happy birthday to you* as you circle the sun.

Rain Rain Go Away

I accidentally swallowed
a cloud—choked
on its puffiness.

Cold rain flooded
my veins—not a damp
sadness like tears fallen
from a child's puffy eyes,
but a frigid emptiness—
a black hole cradling
my small body

before it swallows me—
like I swallowed it—
like we swallow
each other, slowly,

chewing sounds
a lullaby
before silence returns
& I wonder if

it killed me—
if I killed it—
if we killed us.

But saliva
always evaporates
after a storm
as throats stretch
to rainbows—
accordions of scarlets to violets
coating tongues:

the taste of blood
swirled with grape
cough syrup—
the medicinal tingling
of the abyss that lingers
on your dry lips.

The Surrealist Who Could Not Dream

I awaken to birds chirping sirens—
their feathers flash red & blue.
My pillow suffocates me.
I step out of bed with smothered lungs
onto hardwood that splinters
the soles of my feet.
The milk in my fridge is sour. I pour
it into Froot Loops. Their O eyes blink at me.
I take a shower in weeping acid.
The soap bubbles recite dirges.
I break my neck getting out the tub.
I fall asleep in a puddle.

I dream of nothing.
I rest in a coffin
of emptiness.
My Unconscious
sings me a lullaby.
I cannot hear it.

I awaken to a chirping smoke alarm.
It orders me to open my oven.
My head is baking at 350 degrees.
I sigh in relief at the number 5.
I grate my fingertips over my brain,
then stab it with a fork.
I eat it whole.
I slip into a coma.

I dream of nothing.
My Unconscious
curses at me.
I hear static.

I awaken on my balcony—
banister creaking.
I leap.
The pavement catches me.

I dream of nothing.
My Unconscious
is silent.

I awaken to a gun
in my hand.
I fire at my temple.
I watch my limp body
on black & white film.

I dream of nothing.
My Unconscious
sighs.

I awaken to sighing wind.
I feel I've forgotten something.
I hold a knife to my throat.
I hesitate.
I pick up a pen.
I write a poem.

I dream of nothing.
My Unconscious
kisses my forehead.

The Toy War

Childhood's joy land / mystic merry Toyland / once you pass its borders / you can ne'er return again.

— *Toyland*, Doris Day

I gave my teddy bears machine guns—
demanded they drive their tanks

over to my doll collection—
showed them how to rip

their plastic heads off
& waterboard them with cereal milk

until they're gasping for air
& spilling secrets.

The dolls fought back with Barbie-brand knives—
sliced bear bellies open. I let them bleed cotton fluff

on my bedroom carpet—
turned away as they shouted *Traitor!*

unaware my alliance
is only to misery.

The Beanie Babies watched in horror.
I have the power to disembowel them—

skin them alive, mount
their heads on my wall.

But I won't.
I need witnesses.

They've formed a temporary truce—
their common goal: kill me, their god.

& I know we'll die together,
eventually.

& when we're dead,
the Universe will dust off our carcasses—

display us in its museum—
reunited with friends, family, & childhood toys

behind a glass case. Because we're vintage
& must be preserved—

time frozen as we roast
marshmallows over a plastic flame—

in a backyard with plastic grass—
plastic models of our cars parked in the driveway—

in front of our plastic home
that opens its ribs like a dollhouse—

plastic lamps illuminating our memories—
a gold plaque beneath it all that reads simply:

we were here.

Lemonade Stand

Did you know you can make invisible ink
using only lemon juice & heat?
Try this easy recipe!
Fill your pen with lemon juice,
carve a suicide note into your skin—
blend citrus with blood, each pore
a puddle—dab the excess
with a wet Kleenex, swallow
the red evidence. Wait.
Strike a match using your teeth,
then light yourself ablaze:
burning on your pyre,
your flesh will fail to confess
the depression you authored
on your body—scratch & sniff
scarification illegible to onlookers—
a secret diary for an unwell witch
engulfed in fruity gasoline.

Rubber Ducks

float in my Froot Loops—
yellow bodies bobbing
in milk. They flew
to my kitchen—packed
their bags with washcloths
& lavender shampoo
to nest in my dishes.

They say the bathroom is uninhabitable—
the weeping faucet echoes
off acoustic tiles—
the old bloody Band-Aids
that once caulked cut wrists
now drowning
in the stagnant tub—
an outline of my blurry
eyes permanently stamped
on the foggy mirror.

I stir a dairy whirlpool
with my spoon, the ducks
grabbing onto cereal O
life rafts—muffled quacking
inaudible as bubble helmets
swallow their heads.

Popping the bubbles
with my finger,
they cough from the holes
in their bellies—squeeze
out an empty noise:
the toll
of a death
knell ringing
underwater.

Hopscotch With Death

...the abandoned hopscotch courts turn over
one after the other in the sky...

—André Breton

1 pets the Band-Aids sleeping on its wrists.

2 tries to trick its self-esteem with hypnosis—
swings a pocket watch in front of the mirror
to beautify its depressed reflection.

3 sprouts a radio from its chest—spits
static at itself—attempts to block
the ringing with its fingers
but can't escape its own voice.

4 mashes elevator buttons—lights
the plastic like matches
until they combust—fire alarm
coughing ash—the rooftop
still too far from the sparkling stars.

5 is clairvoyant—its cloudy eyes
predicting my future: launching
off a skyscraper, I'll fly—
shove myself from the nest,
the hairs on my arms growing
to feathers—dancing with gravity
as I descend, kissing mist.

6 knocks on camera lenses—
shudders at the sight of passersby
pointing their eyes upward, zoomed-in
pupils magnifying my body like an ant
under a sun beam—gasps
like glittering flashes.

7 rolls its eyes at the commotion—
raises its angry, balled fist
at the traffic jam—wonders why
people have stopped their vehicles—
why they gawk at the sky like sardines
with mouths agape.

8 tells me I'm selfish—
implores me to think
of my family—
to *remember*
god has a plan—
warns me to keep living
if I don't want to burn.

9 calls the ambulance—
tells the press it saw a human
parachute—gives reporters permission
to air the event—to tease the story
before cutting to a black & white spiral
urging viewers to buy new life
insurance policies—to vote now
for a politician promising to cure
the mental illness crisis.

10 forgets my name,
yet staples my limbs
to newspaper headlines.

Detention in Dante's Inferno

So now there ran out of this fractured spigot,
both words and blood.

— *Inferno, Canto XIII*

Because Death would not stop for me,
I leapt in front of his school bus—
cracked my jawbreaker bones
under rolling, starry tires—
rainbow-powdered marrow
dusting an outline
of my soul on the sidewalk.

I stripped him of his black cloak
to dye it pastel pink with my blood,
then bent his scythe into a heart-shaped
choker—its edges shallowly slicing
my throat—painless, eternal.

As I hurriedly opened the iron door,
the principal of Hell
scowled—his horns
piercing detention slips—
his backwards voice
booming:

Your classroom
is downstairs.
Don't run
in the hallways!

My confident steps
turned unsteady
as the spiral staircase
swallowed me—

the abyss salivating
in anticipation
as I reached
the seventh floor.

The classroom was quiet,
filled with murky moonlight.

Glaring with human eyes—
pupils flittering—
the teacher unfolded her wings
as rain poured from the open ceiling—
water dissolving
sticks of chalk—
feathers littering the floor—
her neck a delicate archway
shimmering after a storm.

She tapped
her long acrylic nails
impatiently on the table,
screeching for me to go
to my seat immediately.

In each student desk
sat a barren tree—
their roots
bursting linoleum—
their limbs
drooping
from an invisible weight.

Handing me a pencil
& a piece
of notebook paper,
the teacher instructed
me to infinitely write my sin.

As I began, the pencil
coiled around my
finger
arm
neck
face—
my skull splintering
until branches burst from my brain—
my skin peeling to reveal bark—
my eyes apples rotting worms.

Carve into me my apology—
list the names of everyone
who knew me—
who wipe wet eyes
in the cemetery—
who see my skeleton
strolling under sunlight—
who scorn me for selfishness—
who mourn my mortal form.

Let my body hang with regret—
but let my mind finally rest.

Night Sky Through a Juice Box Straw

We bury ourselves in the park
next to a picnic blanket—
layer dirt & grass atop our limbs,
write *rest in peace* on our foreheads
with magic marker before folding
our fingers over our chests—
daisies draped upon breathing graves.

To plant a tree, one must perform a funeral
for the seed: adorn black gardening gloves,
deliver the eulogy, wield a shovel,
water the soil with sincere tears.

Once we burst through the earth,
are we happy to be saplings—
infant trunks wrapping around
telephone poles, banisters,
passersby's ankles?

Or should we scorn our resurrections—
mourn our suicides—the roots
ripped from the soles of our feet
now placed in glass vases?

We wish our leaves could touch the sun,
but stars hang from our branches like mobiles.

Look at us—our shining apple eyes,
wormholes connecting our brains together.

Look up at the cosmos,
spot the outline of our orchard.

Look through the moon
as if it were the opening of a straw—

as if we were both the child sipping juice at recess
& the contents sloshing inside the carton.

Look down at the ants
that march like constellations,

the ones,

      there,

            carrying our cores on their backs.

Moth Milk

I thought I swallowed moths—
thought I suckled on bottles of eggs
instead of milk—saw their larvae legs
rising like freshly baked cupcake tops
through the window in my stomach—
ready to frost their buttercream wings
with the ding of my kitchen timer—
waiting to taste their first flight up my throat.

They contorted my tongue
into a proboscis—each syllable
a cold breath in closet darkness—
grinding moldy cloth between my teeth—
slipping my neck through coat hanger nooses—
longing to pin my body to a lampshade—
the holes in my heart illuminated
by the bulb burning my exposed back.

But when I switched off the fluorescence—
the warmth of the sun an alarm sounding
through the curtains of my skin—
I instead found butterflies—their golden
wings a crown around my brain—
levitating in a beam of nectar—

the fire I once wanted to die by
burning in my blooming eyes.

Sleepover Seance

Summon me with a Ouija board—
hold hands with your friends in a circle—
light birthday candles with a blowtorch
to accept the terms & conditions
of this seance & forget to hover
your planchette over BYE
before you die
so the next owners of your house
will be stuck
with me too.

Etch me into a locket—lock me
in a safe until you wear me around
your neck during your cruise ship dinner—
oops me into the ocean—
I'll sink into rust
until researchers 84 years later
dredge me from the depths,
deluding themselves in the name of history
into thinking I'm more important
than I truly was.

Convince the coroner I'm art—
to donate me to LACMA—
stuff me with cotton, varnish
me with wax—display me
as a permanent exhibit
gazed upon by a thousand
interpretations.

Throw yourself,
wailing,
over my casket at my funeral—

or just shed a tear at my funeral—

or just attend my funeral—

or just glance at my funeral invitation
before you throw it away—

or just read my obituary from home—

or just know I died—

or just know I was alive—
just please

remember me.

Notes

"Hatching Hot Wheels" and "Cat's Cradle" first appeared in *Sh!t Men Say To Me: A Poetry Anthology in Response to Toxic Masculinity* by Moon Tide Press.

"Be Kind, Please Rewind" borrows its backwards form from Matt Rasmussen's "Reverse Suicide."

"Welcome to the Doll Psych Ward" is inspired by Amy Gerstler's "Touring the Doll Hospital."

"How Many Licks Does It Take to Get to the Center of a Poem?" is a title taken from the Tootsie Pop commercial phrase "How many licks does it take to get to the center of a Tootsie Pop?"

The line "All the world's a stage" from "Sock Puppet Imposter" is from William Shakespeare's *As You Like It*.

"Fragments from a Femme Enfant" is based on the Surrealist trope of the "femme-enfant," where women are simultaneously infantilized, sexualized, and romanticized. The image of fire burning hands is inspired by a scene in *Nadja* by André Breton.

The lines "Because Death would not stop for me / I leapt in front of his school bus" from "Detention in Dante's Inferno" are a modification of Emily Dickinson's lines "Because I could not stop for Death— / He kindly stopped for me—."

The title "Night Sky Through a Juice Box Straw" is inspired by Ocean Vuong's "Night Sky With Exit Wounds."

Acknowledgments

First and foremost, I want to thank Eric Morago and Moon Tide Press for believing in my work throughout the years and for giving me the opportunity to publish this book.

Thank you to Sophie Jane (@LittleNurseGirl) for bringing my book cover vision to life. Your art has inspired me for years and I am so grateful to have had the chance to work with you and your brilliance.

Thank you to all my friends, both my poet friends and my "not-poetry-people" friends, for being loving and encouraging throughout the creation of this book and for being there for me in all other aspects of life.

Thank you to Racy Kaufman for helping me learn about my brain so that I can better express myself and for always believing in my voice.

Thank you to my coworkers at California State University, Dominguez Hills for being supportive and lovely humans and thank you to California State University, Long Beach and my MFA cohort for giving me a space to write my thesis, which would eventually transform into this book. Special thanks to my thesis chair, David Hernandez, for always believing in my work, no matter how weird it got.

Thank you to my parents for always loving and supporting me and for providing me with privileges I do not take for granted. I love you forever.

Thank you to the original Surrealists for creating a movement that inspires me both in art and in life. Though I may stray from the manifesto, I hope the expression of my Unconscious reaches you. Likewise, thank you to the contemporary Pop Surrealists for inspiring me with your creepy-cute pastel metaphors. I don't know if poetry can be considered Pop Surrealist, but I hope this book serves as a love letter to you regardless.

And lastly, thank you, dear reader, for joining me on this surreal adventure. My goal with my work is to connect with you so that we both can feel less alone, and I hope I achieved that, even if only a little. To end with a quote from my favorite Emily Dickinson poem: "I'm Nobody! Who are you? / Are you—Nobody—too? / Then there's a pair of us!"

About the Author

Ally McGregor is a contemporary Surrealist poet from Southern California. She earned both her BA in English Literature and her MFA in Creative Writing (Poetry) from California State University, Long Beach. Her work focuses on womanhood, death, and destigmatizing mental illness. You can find her on Instagram @metaphormannequin.

Also Available from Moon Tide Press

He's a Color Until He's Not, Christian Hanz Lozada (2023)
The Language of Fractions, Nicelle Davis (2023)
Paradise Anonymous, Oriana Ivy (2023)
Now You Are a Missing Person, Susan Hayden (2023)
Maze Mouth, Brian Sonia-Wallace (2023)
Tangled by Blood, Rebecca Evans (2023)
Another Way of Loving Death, Jeremy Ra (2023)
Kissing the Wound, J.D. Isip (2023)
Feed It to the River, Terhi K. Cherry (2022)
Beat Not Beat: An Anthology of California Poets Screwing on the Beat and Post-Beat Tradition (2022)
When There Are Nine: Poems Celebrating the Life an Achievements of Ruth Bader Ginsburg (2022)
The Knife Thrower's Daughter, Terri Niccum (2022)
2 Revere Place, Aruni Wijesinghe (2022)
Here Go the Knives, Kelsey Bryan-Zwick (2022)
Trumpets in the Sky, Jerry Garcia (2022)
Threnody, Donna Hilbert (2022)
A Burning Lake of Paper Suns, Ellen Webre (2021)
Instructions for an Animal Body, Kelly Gray (2021)
Head *V* Heart: New & Selected Poems, Rob Sturma (2021)
Sh!t Men Say to Me: A Poetry Anthology in Response to Toxic Masculinity (2021)
Flower Grand First, Gustavo Hernandez (2021)
Everything is Radiant Between the Hates, Rich Ferguson (2020)
When the Pain Starts: Poetry as Sequential Art, Alan Passman (2020)
This Place Could Be Haunted If I Didn't Believe in Love, Lincoln McElwee (2020)
Impossible Thirst, Kathryn de Lancellotti (2020)
Lullabies for End Times, Jennifer Bradpiece (2020)
Crabgrass World, Robin Axworthy (2020)
Contortionist Tongue, Dania Ayah Alkhouli (2020)
The only thing that makes sense is to grow, Scott Ferry (2020)

Dead Letter Box, Terri Niccum (2019)

Tea and Subtitles: Selected Poems 1999-2019, Michael Miller (2019)

At the Table of the Unknown, Alexandra Umlas (2019)

The Book of Rabbits, Vince Trimboli (2019)

Everything I Write Is a Love Song to the World, David McIntire (2019)

Letters to the Leader, HanaLena Fennel (2019)

Darwin's Garden, Lee Rossi (2019)

Dark Ink: A Poetry Anthology Inspired by Horror (2018)

Drop and Dazzle, Peggy Dobreer (2018)

Junkie Wife, Alexis Rhone Fancher (2018)

The Moon, My Lover, My Mother, & the Dog, Daniel McGinn (2018)

Lullaby of Teeth: An Anthology of Southern California Poetry (2017)

Angels in Seven, Michael Miller (2016)

A Likely Story, Robbi Nester (2014)

Embers on the Stairs, Ruth Bavetta (2014)

The Green of Sunset, John Brantingham (2013)

The Savagery of Bone, Timothy Matthew Perez (2013)

The Silence of Doorways, Sharon Venezio (2013)

Cosmos: An Anthology of Southern California Poetry (2012)

Straws and Shadows, Irena Praitis (2012)

In the Lake of Your Bones, Peggy Dobreer (2012)

I Was Building Up to Something, Susan Davis (2011)

Hopeless Cases, Michael Kramer (2011)

One World, Gail Newman (2011)

What We Ache For, Eric Morago (2010)

Now and Then, Lee Mallory (2009)

Pop Art: An Anthology of Southern California Poetry (2009)

In the Heaven of Never Before, Carine Topal (2008)

A Wild Region, Kate Buckley (2008)

Carving in Bone: An Anthology of Orange County Poetry (2007)

Kindness from a Dark God, Ben Trigg (2007)

A Thin Strand of Lights, Ricki Mandeville (2006)

Sleepyhead Assassins, Mindy Nettifee (2006)

Tide Pools: An Anthology of Orange County Poetry (2006)

Lost American Nights: Lyrics & Poems, Michael Ubaldini (2006)

Patrons

Moon Tide Press would like to thank the following people for their support in helping publish the finest poetry from the Southern California region. To sign up as a patron, visit www.moontidepress.com or send an email to publisher@moontidepress.com.

Anonymous
Robin Axworthy
Conner Brenner
Nicole Connolly
Bill Cushing
Susan Davis
Kristen Baum DeBeasi
Peggy Dobreer
Kate Gale
Dennis Gowans
Alexis Rhone Fancher
HanaLena Fennel
Half Off Books & Brad T. Cox
Donna Hilbert
Jim & Vicky Hoggatt
Michael Kramer
Ron Koertge & Bianca Richards
Gary Jacobelly
Ray & Christi Lacoste
Jeffery Lewis
Zachary & Tammy Locklin
Lincoln McElwee
David McIntire
José Enrique Medina
Michael Miller & Rachanee Srisavasdi
Michelle & Robert Miller
Ronny & Richard Morago
Terri Niccum
Andrew November
Jeremy Ra
Luke & Mia Salazar
Jennifer Smith
Roger Sponder
Andrew Turner
Rex Wilder
Mariano Zaro
Wes Bryan Zwick

Made in the USA
Middletown, DE
18 February 2024

49384938R00059